The University of Wisconsin Press

Angela Sorby

BIRD SKIN COAT

The University of Wisconsin Press
1930 Monroe Street, 3rd Floor
Madison, Wisconsin 53711–2059

www.wisc.edu/wisconsinpress/

3 Henrietta Street
London WC2E 8LU, England

5   4   3   2   1

Printed in the United States of America

Library of Congress Cataloging-in-Publication Data
Sorby, Angela.
  Bird skin coat / Angela Sorby.
      p. cm. — (The Brittingham prize in poetry)
  Poems.
  ISBN 978-0-299-23190-3 (hardcover : alk. paper) — ISBN 978-0-299-23194-1
  (pbk. : alk. paper) — ISBN 978-0-299-23193-4 (e-book)
  I. Title. II. Series: Brittingham prize in poetry (Series)
  PS3619.O73B57 2009
  811'.6—dc22
                              2008038492

BIRD SKIN COAT

THE BRITTINGHAM PRIZE IN POETRY

To three doves:
Ivan
Jonah
Francesca

Birdskin clothes are light, warm and waterproof, but they tear easily. On arrival in the Department of Conservation, the skin of the parka was torn in several places. With ageing, the feathers had become less securely attached to the skin and were easily dislodged. The tears were repaired by adhering patches of a Japanese tissue paper coloured to match, or where possible with goldbeaters' skin, a transparent membrane prepared from ox intestine, which more closely matches the appearance of the skin. The parka was then gently padded with acid-free tissue paper. However, the parka remains fragile, and cannot be exhibited, because this might lead to further damage and loss of feathers.

COLLECTION NOTE, DEPARTMENT OF CONSERVATION, BRITISH MUSEUM, LONDON

CONTENTS

ACKNOWLEDGMENTS

Poems from this collection first appeared in the following journals, sometimes in an earlier form:

National Poetry Review: "Sky Falling on Cedars," "Whose Woods These Are"

Pinyon: "Catch and Release," "Transport to Sumer"

Portland Review: "Insomnia," "The Attic of the Attic"

Seattle Review: "The Snow-Woman"

Southern Review: "Bird Skin Coat," "Breathing Out Smoke,"
  "Nostalgia for the Present"

Sycamore Review: "Dove and Dove"

Third Coast: "What Helen Caught"

Willow Springs: "Six Degrees of Separation"

Zone 3: "Mountain of Names"

For feedback on earlier drafts, I wish to thank Maureen McLane; my writing group (Jenny Benjamin-Smith, Colleen Harryman, Liana Odrcic, and Melissa Schoeffel); and I. H. Roth. For other forms of support, I am grateful to my colleagues at Marquette University. I am also deeply indebted to Janice Anderson, Sandra Lee Kleppe, Chris Roth, Janet and Evan Sorby, and Tracy Thompson.

PART ONE

BIRD SKIN COAT

Two Toyotas crash.
No real damage. The drivers
are blessed
              by the pope of fate,
the one who appears erratically,
the one who doesn't shave.

Their engines purr *ho hum*
ho hum, awry on offramp ice.
Do the drivers deserve
their down coats?
                    The wind
says *heck if I know*.
It can't reach their bones.

The man's airbags blew: he's okay,
just bloody with small flesh
wounds.
          The woman he hit
is still 42. She notes with wonder
how her parka fits her perfectly
the way a dove's skin holds
the whole bird together.
                          Fate
is not a thing with feathers,
it's old, bald, and blind,
a pope who can't decipher
the man's name,
              David Pratt,
as he scrawls it on scratch paper.
But the woman reads: *David*,
Yahweh's beloved. She has never felt safer.

BREATHING OUT SMOKE

C'est l'Ennui!—l'oeil chargé d'un pleur involontaire,
Il rêve d'échafauds en fumant son houka.
Tu le connais, lecteur, ce monstre délicat,
—Hypocrite lecteur,—mon semblable,—mon frère!
CHARLES BAUDELAIRE, "AU LECTEUR"

On Day 110 of W.'s second term
I join my neighbor, Caddie,

on her porch, where she folds
her leggy black-Irish go-to-hell

body into a wicker rocker and fires
up a Pall Mall. Long ago, in junior high,

football stars threw pennies in gym
yelling *scrounge* at special-ed kids.

This seemed natural—inevitable—
part of the fixed Linnaean order.

But now our rust belt city's so rusty
it's falling to pieces, like Caddie's car

that coughs when she turns the key.
Why quit smoking? Smoke's

our cityscape, our V of geese at dusk.
My mom says we've got no class,

because our kids run on the lawn in socks.
Their uncut bangs half-block their view

of our other neighbor—Pearl—whose helmet
shields her during seizures. She's fifty-six,

too young to wander like she wanders.
But maybe to be seized is to flower,

like the *Linneaus borealis* that spreads
from Northern clime to clime,

blooming in sync with summer,
blanketing boreal woods with its petals,

as if there were no hierarchical order,
as if the rivulets were clear,

as if the Canada geese could bring us
word from the birch and the silver fir:

     mon semblable, we wish
they'd say, or squawk. *Ma soeur*.

NOSTALGIA FOR THE PRESENT

The mansion on Wisconsin Avenue's been restored, like royalty brought back
to England after the plague. One look at the bright brass knobs and it's clear:
all the rats here are dead. "And *voilà*, the coffee room!" the realtor says, opening
a glass door. I'm a fake, of course, nodding speculatively as if I just happened

to have a half-million to blow on nine bedrooms and three bathrooms,
as if I could bathe in more than one tub at a time. But I do want my bed
to be invisible at breakfast, with my spoons stored far from my shoes:
distances ensure that waking and walking can proceed apace, that my life,

unlike my apartment, hasn't collapsed into a small dense cube of time
and space. Better not to know too much physics, I want to tell the realtor.
Better not to know who lived in this house before it was restored,
when it was adrift in the world between the wars. The rich

are exactly like you and me, only their house is empty and the rings
where the cat's cream sat has been sanded away. And their house
will outlive us all; it is richer than any human portfolio, basking in the luxury
of silence, of limestone pulled from mines in Indiana. Go to Indiana

and the holes remain: filled with water like the pools Zen monks use

to reflect on the poverty of matter.

ROSE

i.
Milwaukee Avenue, 2006,
and the lone rose insists:

Red! Rose-Red!
But the little girl

on the trike plows
past—she's all about Disney:

Snow White, Sleeping Beauty.
The girl is half-watched

by three teen dads
who could be brothers.

Soon the rose will draw
its shades, a failed enterprise,

and its bee will buzz
into the sky. The three

dads will storm Garibaldi's,
flashing forged IDs.

The girl's dad drinks
pale ale. When he sings

he's embarrassing.
No one's ear cocks,

and the noise level
rises—not just sports

chatter, not TV,
but a deep roar pouring

like sewage under the street.
It keeps overflowing

into Lake Michigan,
until the bay clouds

and gulls falter. The dad
bobs. He wavers. He's too drunk

to hold his voice close,
so it goes. Mouthing Johnny Cash

it ups and leaves,

      catching and lodging

with all the empty
plastic bags in the trees.

ii.
I went down, down, down
in a burning ring of fire,

down to the sewer
where the goldfish gleam:

they are not pets. Their spines
flex like little mermaids,

like creatures in a sleeping
girl's dream. The rose has learned

its lesson: *hush. Don't deepen,*
don't redden, keep still

like a bead of water
in an enchanted

state without hills.

WHOSE WOODS THESE ARE

The alderman leaflets:
a REGISTERED SEX OFFENDER
is living in the duplex on the corner,
buttering toast (inoffensively?)
while the old Shakespearian wheel of fortune
falls off a passing Camry.

"You're out," says Pat Sajak
on TV. Health and Safety,
two tarted-up twins,
roll into a ditch full of phlox.
The phlox resists abstraction.
It doesn't give a flying F

about the state of the union.
Undo the duplex and it's simplex:
a sore point beyond good and evil,
a LUV U license plate hammered out
by felons. The fall trees leaflet leaves,
their red veins psychedelic

with rot and wild weather.
I see his house from here:
our grave Offender. His roof
shelters him like a mother,
but the storms are neuromuscular—

dark and deep—

the storms are in our bodies as we sleep.

NEIGHBORHOOD WATCH

Insomnia's a ring twisting
around my fourth finger

as the tree outside my window
scratches and hacks like Edith Piaf's

cat—the one that outlived her.
Its rasps aren't French

but something stranger
like the purrs Ojibwes heard

when Père Marquette first prayed
among the birches.

Now Milwaukee's churches
are dead after ten

except for the cats that slip
into St. John's cathedral

and sniff the carpet,
seeking comestible life,

while the body of Christ waits,
crispy and scentless

in cellophane under the altar.
I lost my faith in 1985

for no reason. It was like falling
out of a tree: I lay there panting

but my neck wasn't broken.
I could still wiggle my feet.

So now all my windows open
into the same ambivalent semi-detached

darkness. If this neighborhood
has a patron saint, let's say

it's the retired science teacher
who paces Kinnickinnic Avenue

using two sticks to keep a third
aloft. Sometimes he walks for hours

practicing his trick, which, like a purr
or prayer, has no clear point.

I drifted through science class,
learning zip about cells and seeds,

but I know that two blocks east
the Kinnickinnic River weeps

and weeps, its cargo dead frogs,
fish, and rats, all pale with PCBs.

Milwaukee, Wisconsin's so densely
human it flushes its toxins back

through the water supply,
and yet we're neighbors, the river and I,

locked in currents that make us
endangered and dangerous,

part of the same junkie body
that buzzes and flashes all night,

under stars that shiver, dropping
dirty needles of light.

SMALL TALK

We're strangers chatting
about stormy weather
as the elevator whisks us to the top
of the U.S. Bank Building,
but not higher, no never

higher

though we aspire
to rise above ourselves in flocks
like lost Canada geese.
Their goose hearts beat together.
They are not afraid to cry in public:
We are too many!
We are weeds!
And yet though lost we fly fearlessly
over Milwaukee.

O strangers in the lift,
don't hold my gaze. It is enough
to know you are too close
for comfort. Fellow citizens
of America's fattest state,
it is not weight that keeps us
down, but heart trouble:

blockages, skips, little *ifs*.
The weather is not small. It is larger
than we are, larger than North
America (*avec* Canada),
perhaps co-terminal with God and Allah,

so let us small-talk

in the hushed tones of nuns and lovers,
as we unzip our coats
and shake off the drops.
We can't feel fully human
when we're wet. Such is the rain's gift.
Such is the rain's largesse.

MIDDLE DISTANCE

The neighborhood husbands
drive en masse to Ames,
trailing van emissions, gone
like princes turned to swans.

Why? Why Ames?

For baseball, they say. They leave
and we picture sewn-up white leather,
a head with no face, an orb aloft,

a sun.

Whack. Home run. The ball sails
out of the park. It falls in tall grass.
It nests though it's no swan.

Later, the drunk men tumble
to bed at a Holiday Inn. Too beat
for CNN, they snore, then breathe
their snores back in.
                              To know all:
in *Paradise Lost*, that was Satan's
first sin. But Iowa's not Eden—

in dreams we women watch
the stadium's roof roll up.
Is it motorized? Do we care?
Our pillows smell of aloe, like our hair.

Husbandly bodies are prairies
where grasses seed grasses,

spreading endlessly,

up to—and over—the edge
of intelligibility. Is Iowa far?
Yes and no—its borders are unclear

after sundown, when the corn grows:
we are *here*,
and our husbands are *there*,

as if a distinction could be made
between the plain Midwestern night
and ghostlier demarcations,
deeper shades.

ERIN'S LEATHER JACKET

The arborist's wife, Erin, will be beautiful
at fifty: her beauty is so pale, so blonde, it floats independently
of her face, like the "spirits" that nineteenth-century fakes
brushed onto daguerreotypes. I barely know her, so she disarms me
when she asks, "Why are you wearing such a flashy ring?"
My ring has four diamonds. Four big diamonds. They stick
out like Jayne Mansfield's breasts in a 1950s boned bra.
In 1954, before I was born, my grandfather traded an acre
lot at Martha Lake for these gems. They lay loose
in his safety deposit box until after his death. A diamond
is nothing like a breath. "Diamonds are forever" say the ads,
but what they don't say is, "Forever doesn't matter."
I need time to weed and water. Erin's house
is too close. Her coat is brushed leather. Her boys
are my boys' ages: two and five. Our boys are doppelgängers.
"Why are you wearing such a flashy ring?"

                                        Erin, listen:
I like the way it bites my other fingers as I fall asleep.
It whispers a little nonsense about an acre on a lake.
I'm forty, not beautiful and I won't age beautifully,
but the lake is the exact temperature of a human
body—as if we could both plunge in—
as if our cells were porous, not sewn

                              up so fast in skin.

DRAGONS OF THE BIBLE

And the parched ground shall become a pool, and the thirsty land
springs of water; in the habitation of dragons, where each lay,
shall be grass with reeds and rushes.
ISAIAH 35:7

Their scales are hidden
deeper than any Sumerian grave,
deeper than ice-age silver veins,

in the world God couldn't bring
himself to make.

We find their ghosts in the clouds:

blank, shifty, enormous.

Dragons never join us
on Wisconsin's wet surface,
where it's humid all summer,
as if someone—or something—
large were breathing

the herbs to life.
Our mint multiplies

as dragons drift

on the cusp of heat,
but never quite flesh.
We don't want our necks
torn up, though we tell ourselves

we're exceptional—that if they descend,
they'll see us as kin,
since our lungs are grey with smoke
from oil and coal.
Somewhere God ends—

and there dragons spread
their wings like a living

Bible in the dark sky
over the light sky
over our heads.

WALKING DIRECTIONS

Never take the street
if there's an alley:
a cracked crevice
between blocks,
where bodies are tactile, not visible,
and losing even vital
organs feels natural,
spurred by a stubborn

immortal streak

that keeps us up
all hours like cats.
The alley's edged
in chain-link yards
that strain blurrily

against the night

bird in his muscle

shirt who sings
neither roses nor weeds.
He won't name the route—
what he wants is whistling

between our teeth:

a swerve off key,
into the map's damp crease.
If there's an alley, friend,
don't take the street.

WHAT HELEN CAUGHT

On Sophie Freud's death-day
her lungs filled like two Austrian crystal

tumblers—costly, frail, see-through—
and then they collapsed, dashed

not by some hysterical bride
but by a virus that passed

through her palms and into her blood.
It took two more weeks for the flu

to find the Andersons, Seattle Swedes
unconscious of the unconscious.

On Henry Anderson's death-day
his lungs sputtered like a Model T.

His father (my great-grandfather)
closed his eyes. Henry's engine

powered the house: it heated
the cellar. It lit the porch.

Why couldn't his sister Helen die
instead? No one spoke

these words: instead the question
fell on the house like a raven's shadow,

and the bedrooms got so cold
that Helen (my grandmother) lost

half her hair: it disappeared,
into a black bird's nest.

Meanwhile, Sophie's father
revised his book on dreams:

in dreams the world is germfree—
danderless dogs, twins in gloves,

pure wells. Drink the waters
of sleep, he preached.

But some old houses can't hold
heat. Even in summer the chill leaks

through the children's bed
linens. In 1918, in Seattle,

everything was communicable:
Helen caught her father's

       disappointment

like a wedding bouquet. Teens,
twenties, eighties, nineties—

she inhaled its lilac scent
every day, and it never failed her,

and she slept with it under her pillow
because she loved her father.

CATCH AND RELEASE

My mom's mom and dad
barely spoke to each other.
Their fights smolder silently
behind our family snapshots
from the sixties and seventies,
as if every Christmas were a tree on fire.
Death didn't bring them closer. His heaven
is silver, like the inside of a thermos,
or the fields of lower Rainier,
while hers is radishes cut to look like roses.
Nothing I can say is fully true. Every family
holds its secrets until it turns blue.
One thing's for sure: blue's not the word
for their black-and-white hands, held, hers in his,
for a camera in 1940. They're posed
in front of five dead fish, but these can't serve
as metaphors. Instead I want to know more
about the luminous wall behind them:
whose house was it? Was dinner delicious?
What time did they turn in?
                          So, 1940:
after dinner they climb the stairs to a guest room.
No one knows it's there; it just grows
as rooms do in dreams. I want to watch them
from above. I want to hold my breath and watch
my grandparents make love.

CONVERSION NARRATIVE

When Mount Rainier comes out we're taken in
by its vast calm—the calm of a corrupt spiritual leader—
and I remember Elizabeth Clare Prophet's skin
(how luminous, how light) as she predicted the end
of the world from a podium at the Holiday Inn.
And now another grandmother's lost all speech,
and the end of the world edges closer,
blank and elemental as a glacier.

    A stroke: it sounds pacific,

as Rainier looks pacific in the broad March light.
The atmosphere magnifies the Pass
and the Muir snowfield with its hikers' boots
and bones in every crevasse. There are many paths
from Paradise Lodge to the mountaintop,
paths we Anderson women won't follow,
with our tricky knees and our vertigo.
Still, I think Rainier will come to us

when I am her age and we meet in dreams

unable to talk or touch. The summit will deliver
its thin air, unfolding acres of whiteness,
as if death were nothing but a shared view
of all that escapes us.

MOUNTAIN OF NAMES

I'm bad with names, so as I push forty,
I forgive myself for hiking lower Rainier

past lots of biggish, greyish birds

that I can't describe more precisely.
Tit for tat: the birds don't know
my species name, either, *Homo sapiens*,
nor my "common" moniker, *Angela*,
which means "messenger from God,"
nor are they aware of my medicinal uses,
spelled out on my organ donor card.

It's a spring day, dizzy with ignorance.

The ash in this meadow's volcanic (I guess)
except for the one-tenth of one percent
that used to be my grandmother.
We scattered her here with no marker,
and field guides don't list her new name,

now that she's crossed over
from the humanities to the sciences.
        Is ash a mineral?
Is death implicit in the periodic table?
If I could coin a word for this meadow,
part grandmother, part volcano, I'd keep mum.
The mountain's most itself when darkness
veils its glacier, the way key messages

transmit themselves,

sans messenger.

THE SNOW-WOMAN

Her body's weighty, two snow-balls,
and so white she leeches red paint from the sled.
The whole yard resembles her: white getting whiter
as if it were all in her head.

Yesterday she fell in a trance from the sky.

I gave her buttons and two coal eyes.
She is an ambassador from the Old Order,
from the ice force that carved out the Kettle Moraine.
Her mineral rights are clear: she shares the past
with the stars and carries a stillness so vast it moves
like a glacier across the yard.
She asks nothing of me. I ask nothing in return.
I am genetically closer to mushrooms
than to her. Her roots are elsewhere, like the roots
of the daughter I will never bear,
and so things settle between us.

THE DIAGNOSIS

It's genetic:
my son's a fire-walker.
His thumbs limbo
backwards. His brain
smokes and stutters.

Other boys
are fire-tenders.
Look how they earn
their scout badges,
leaning sticks to make a tiny
tepee: brush and tinder.

A *fire-walker*,
whisper the normal
moms in normal jeans.
Their pens click.
They X his name
off their kid-party
guest lists.

They are totally. Fucking. Meticulous.

What can I do but coax
him over the embers?
And if he cries (he will)
I'll say *walk faster*.

INSOMNIA

I'm not surprised to find myself awake.
I want to dial dead people long distance:
Tante Kitty, Sheila Bender, David Lee.
My husband is breathing evenly, his skin
a sleeping bag zipped around his chin.
In the daytime, too, he moves with an ease
that is not contagious. Be happy, he says,
as if giving directions for plain paper
recycling.
        I hear Dick Van Dyke
on the downstairs neighbor's TV,
but no one's awake down there.
Before Thomas Edison taped
himself singing "Mary's Lamb,"
the human voice was tethered to the body,
like a falcon on a leash. If a whisperer
whispered, his throat was inches away,
emitting scent and heat.
        Once, years ago,
my grandfather talked me to sleep. He talked
about roofing and siding, roofing and siding.
This much the dead can tell me: sleepers aren't solitary.
There are so many, and they sleep so intently.

PART TWO

KICKFLIP

The middle-aged man's
young man floats
under the surface of his skin,
visible via acne scars,
visible via skateboarders skating

through half-pipes
that turn them into new
skateboarders who in turn
turn into others—hit hit hit. If I squint
I see all the boys who smashed

into walls at fifteen.
They sleep beneath
the I-5 bridge like bats,
dark, fuzzy, jittery, moving
in ruts their muscles remember.

There's an endless supply
of skateboarders, so why
do they look familiar,
as if the world were lazily
recycling the same twelve guys?

Their wheels hum like bees,
as if buzz could make the soul
mobile, though even Christ
had to leave his human hands
behind. And at dusk the black

and blue flies outdo everyone,
ascending like pupils
from the dilated eyes
of scabby itchy witnesses
trying to stay high.

THE ATTIC OF THE ATTIC

for E.

i. Apostrophe
1982: these are house numbers, and we live here together,
and as the snow hits our roof it turns tender. We're sealed off
from ourselves growing older: our room's at the top

of a ladder we've kicked over. If the downstairs burns,
we'll rise, languid as bong water, closing our eyes, and the darkness
will save us. Where will you be when the snow stops falling

and Ronald Reagan forgets to tie his shoes? This attic
is the attic of every room I will ever walk through: I'll tilt one ear
at the ceiling and hear myself talking to you.

ii. Chorus
In Attica, that fiery flower, Western Civ made itself matter—
Now Athens can't rid itself of ruins; feral cats
redouble their numbers but no one can tell
which are ghosts and which are real,
and it's not on the 101 exam:
fur or sham? F either way.
The cats know: smart
or stoned, our words
are arena-rock
inane

because we are not cats,
and because we've never been hungry.

PROSPERITY

*For the Real, whatever upheaval we subject it to, is always and in every case
in its place; it carries its place stuck to the sole of its shoe, there being nothing
that can exile it from it.*
JACQUES LACAN, *ÉCRITS*

Turn off the stereo: the record slows in suave turns like a boy
who knows his strength. Once in the Age of Vinyl, heat

warped Led Zeppelin beyond salvation. The rec room ceiling
carpet matched the floor. Our parents wrote notes:

Please excuse my child as she is flying to Sun Valley.
Nothing mattered. We jumped from tree to tree.

*Please excuse my child as she is simian and may regress
to an earlier stage of evolution.* My friend Thompson

locked himself in the golf course shed with a revolver.
(*Please excuse me as I'm not a child,* but what's this stereo

doing playing all scratches and scars?) "Listen, loser,"
I said through the golf shed door, "don't you know how lucky

you are?" But there were no meters, no markers, no maps.
Far off in France, Jacques Lacan sketched the Real in dense

prose meant to fend off readers. He chewed his hand-
rolled cigarette. *The Real is the state of nature we have lost*

by our fall into language. But here's what's weirder:
as I waited for Thompson, I held my own hand like a lover,

as if it mattered—palm, fingers, thumb. "You've never even
had sex," I hissed, and he dropped the gun.

FLYOVER STATE

Madame Blavatsky, the fraudulent
founder of modern theosophy,
prevaricated blithely, claiming
Jesus reached the Himalayas.
He didn't suffer altitude sickness.
Ascent (she said) was in his blood.
He came down holier
than he went up.
                    In 1994
when my Sanskritist flatmate
shot up, he went to Blavatsky's peaks—
not the real Himalayas but the fakes
painted on fin-de-siècle screens. Our kitchen
smelled of barf and needle-bleach,
so after dark I'd walk outside
down Greenwood Avenue
under lushly brainy blooming trees.
My Doc Martens stamped
ahead of me. My empty shoulder hurt
where its book bag should be.
        And always,
flying low, like a raven:
my half-done dissertation.
The university's spires flared,
lit by lights meant to scare
black teenagers. Its mock-Oxford
turrets acted older than they were.
If I walked all the way to the quad,
my key-card would admit me.
        So instead I looped
around 52nd to Woolworth's,
where the cashiers, Ruth and Rotunda,
let half-price parakeets fly
free among the shoppers.
Woolworth's was the opposite
of history, its liquids and plastics

on the verge of being swept
into some stranger's future
suitcase, shower, tragedy—who could say?

Blavatsky was right: truth mattered less

and less every day, and the discount
parakeets, green with scabby claws,

moved downward to darkness

behind racks of inexplicably
gigantic white bras. Who could fill
such cups? Is there no God but God?

TAJ MAHAL

The yoga teacher's bones are pure
as unbleached cotton, the stuff
of yoga mats, as if she builds
herself from scratch
every Tuesday at the Y.
The teacher moves from Cat
to Downward Facing Dog, reminding me
that India's a real place where strays
outnumber pets. When my cousin Beth
came back from the Assembly of God
Mission Station in Calcutta,
she was light as a straw hat,
and scary-skinny. I wondered if Jesus
would ever give her heart back.
She brought me a soapstone Taj Mahal,
but she didn't want to talk,
though she promised to "keep me
in her prayers."

    How could I say *no thanks?*

Some Tuesdays when I fail
to touch my head to my knees,
Beth veers into view, a cousin
drowning in the burning Ganges,
a grown girl whose DNA is shorn
of its human strands, like an angel
in a cathedral, the kind with blank
stone eyeballs. If I do yoga for weeks,
my hands will finally reach my toes
and I'll know what I already know:
prayers aren't cages, tombs, or fridges,
and no one can keep us there,
because we're—all of us—moving
from Dog to Bird to Air.

AMERICAN CAMEL

In 1859 orders were received for a contingent at Camp Verde to ready twenty-four camels to explore the unknown territory of the Big Bend region of Texas. The absence of sufficient water had defeated many an expedition into the desolate and arid land. The camels seemed to have an uncanny ability to find water at just the right time. On one stretch the caravan traveled 110 miles in almost four days without water—much to the astonishment of the military superiors.
KEN KNAPP, "THE CAMELS OF CAPE VERDE"

i.
On Fridays we walked,
Bryan and Mark and me,
behind the L-shaped stadium,
talking about the kids
from our high school
who put Nick Drake
on their car stereo and drove
off a bridge. Two deaths:
glam, we agreed.

    Above our heads,
the national anthem
was both flat and sharp.
The crowd roared
like a rocket taking off,
though God knows
the stadium stayed put.
It stayed for the long haul,
its bent L the beginning
of some grander word:
Lorca, Laceration, Lariat—

or maybe not.

Maybe its L was the start
of a long silence, and the crowd
was a cover story

for loss after loss,
for camels imported to settle the West,
later sold to circuses,

later still shrunk and stuck

on packs of cigarettes
smoked by kids
who didn't cheer the team,
who couldn't picture their own hands
gleaming in the pockets
of their preshrunk jeans.

ii.
Repeat after me,
the camel croaks:
knuckles aren't humps.
But he lacks credibility. Look
how awkwardly he stumbles,
knocked off-kilter
by water welling weirdly
on his spine. Look how he changes
the landscape until the hills
aren't hills and the sky's
not sky. How can an actual animal
so closely resemble a lie?

SKY FALLING ON CEDARS

All our winged thoughts turn to poultry.
HENRY DAVID THOREAU, "WALKING"

When I Google my dad on the Web
his name pops up on poultry.com,
where he warns fellow chicken-hobbyists

to bring them indoors during storms.
If it's pouring in Seattle,
my dad curls up with his chickens,

Gertie and Maude. The fireplace roars.
Gas licks the fake logs. Thor, the Norse God
of Thunder, has fallen asleep in his book—

he's fictive now, and his kingdom's
a welfare democracy. Memo to self:
nobody's dad can move the earth and sky.

The Cascades sprang from plate tectonics,
oysters co-evolved with tides, and who can say
why bark peels off the live madrona trees?

When my dad visits me in Milwaukee,
he tries to fix things, nailing down
the warping windowsills. Once he installed

a shower with its hot and cold handles
reversed. The fiberglass stall's so small
it makes me concentrate. I wash my hair

mindfully, standing stock-still and alone
in my body, while all around me water
falls like rain on the Pacific coast

two thousand miles away. I rinse my brain
into an avian state: poultry.com,
with its maps of safe bird shelters.

Still, I know when the big quake
hits Seattle, Gertie and Maude will rise
above their splintering coop,

blazing red and gold, Blake-angels
prophesying *cluck*. Translation: *petals,*
meteors, shingles, shit, love—what falls falls

half in grass, half in mud. Feathers & skin,
we glimmer bright but dumb
in the darting jittery random alien sun.

SLEEPING WITH STARS

At the Ditto Tavern in 1990,
nights were blurry copies of copies,
speakers and woofers,
and bass lines repeated themselves
like angry cops. Damn, you were tan:
you took off your Sub Pop T backstage,
and its ghost remained, a torso, like that freaky
Winged Victory in the Louvre.
Your forearms, neck, and face were brown,
and wrinkles waited in the wings of your smooth
cool skin. Oh, yes, you were cool.
(Your weight: 110. Your boyfriend: grunge
musician.) Your coolness coated me
in sunblock—the kind that wears off in an hour.

So friend, it's 2005, and we're semi-old ladies,
and Stephen Hawking says black holes
don't obliterate matter (or if they do, it's not forever)—
so let's barge backwards and march our girl
selves down to the ferry terminal where Seattle's
not cool, just rainy. Your tan fades. Your knuckles
turn pale and salty. The stars are lost in veils
of mist. You can't orient yourself celestially.
Now will you take my hand at last?
Now will you look at me?

FOREST FLOOR

Stille be thou, Sathanas!
The ys fallen ambes aas.
Wendest thou ich were ded for noht?
ANON., *THE HARROWING OF HELL*, CA. 1300

The winter I was twenty,
I fell in love with James,

an animate isolate who read
medieval miracle plays
in a basement so wet

that slugs crossed the floor,
slower than slow sex.
They carried essential elements
(water? darkness? DNA?)
in bodies that doubled as heads.

We lay damp in bed

while upstairs, James's dad,
a famous conservationist,

drank whiskey and typed, working
all day in scary-huge white
men's briefs. Never pants.

James said he dreamed
of knowing only dead languages,

so he wouldn't have to talk
to his father. Their house

smelled like a long hike:
cedar, smoke, and sweat,
and their land went on for miles
of Douglas fir.

The space heater burned red
as an allegorical Satan—
luxuriant with pollution.

The father banged his keys:
Dear Senator Murray,
Dear Senator Gorton,

as we lay there
underground,

unforgiven.

SLEEPING IN THE PIONEER ROOMS

Prince Rupert, British Columbia

The dark has many colors. None are black,
the way the sea is never black but blue,
a blue that drowns the night but stays afloat
like sailors' missing fingers—drifting—do.
My near-love's hair is salt and sweat asleep:
I breathe it in, it turns a deeper hue
of seal, of roe, of fisher cold and sleek,
all tones we cannot touch but, touching, make.
We take the Inside Passage, heading north,
like Haida rowers rowing far from shore—
arms sore but pushing forward with a force
as blind and wet as water under oars.
Near-love, our love's an ebb and flow of sea
that, rushing out, pulls darkness into me.

OBJECTS MADE REAL BY OBSERVATION

for T. R. T.

Ignis fatuus: swamp light illuminates
the frogs, to their distress.
"Miracles are monsters," Emerson
preached, and the frogs concur
in chorus—they prefer darkness.
"I flew once," says my chemist
friend as we walk our loop,
"just inches off the ground."
Quantum physics proves the sidewalk's
mostly empty space,
neither flat nor round.

O frogs of night, we're sick
of losing weight. We want mud
to stick to our boots. Our feet
should leave prints on cement,
as if the swamp were tracking us,
as if the earth were urgently
desirous of our company. But boys
in cars have stopped shouting,
and we pass unobserved
like subatomic particles smashing
the laws of the known world.

NIGHT TRAIN TO WHITEFISH

1988. The Whitefish ski train owes no debt
to Hitchcock. Its strangers are explicable,
neither mysterious nor criminal.
Their lift tags dangle from their zippers. They doze
and dream a predictable jumble of trig exams and sex.
They're uniformly twenty.

Outside, the snow does its best
        to blow a hole in the train.

The doctor forbade this trip since I have shingles,
"an illness commonest in women over eighty,"
and though I'm only twenty,
pain upholsters me
with tiny tacks.
                Still, I swear: all week I'll ski
powder acres where the snow heals fast,
closing around my tracks. I'll take this pain
and carry it lightly,
as if my old self,
age eighty,

were strapped to my back:

she rests her chin on my shoulder

and coaxes me down the hill.

IN THE GOOD PAIN WING

Screams fill
the room with cave smell:
Lascaux bison straining
in opposite directions,

still attached. The Cro-Magnon
artist blurred their backs,
smudging them together,
the way a mother

mixes tetchy DNA
into her newborn's veins.

                              Later,
the mother waits for love to land,
but even this is not effortless:
it circles awkwardly,
an *ichthyornis*, its pale,
keeled breastbone pulling
strength from isolation.

The bed's unmade.
Its stiff waves crinkle,
a wine-dark sea, the Odyssey's
inaugural dactyl,

but the floor is salty—unsteady—
and the baby's eyes stare,
trout-flat.

Love. Love. When will it land?

The child falls asleep. The mother bleeds
until she's too weak to open
the window. Then she opens
the window.

SIX DEGREES OF SEPARATION

Alice B. Toklas was alive in 1966,
but my parents (being themselves) were absorbed
in buying diapers, paying rent, blowing up
        the blow-up pool—
so it didn't dawn on them that if
they dropped everything
(golf clubs, keys, oven mitts)
and flew Pan Am to Paris,
and rented a mini,

they could find Alice B. at her flat in France,
resplendent in a black wool dress,
marinating half a lamb,
and they could set me on her lap.
Most laps are chairs—dull and sturdy—
but hers would be itchy and dense
like a college lecture
in twentieth-century history,
and her hands would be cold,
betraying a lingering

nostalgia for the Vichy puppet state.
But we missed our chance. Alice is dead,
and so is Freud, so there's no one to say
that my parents (*mother especially*) are to blame.
        Every life is its own flame.

And now, in the summer of 2003,
George Bush is peddling a "road map to peace,"
and Eminem is touring, and the world teems
with historical figures that my son will never meet.
Just today, Gregory Peck died. And where were we?
We were sitting on a tilted picnic bench
in Milwaukee.

        Son, I'm sorry.
The sex-ed books call birth a miracle,
but what they don't describe is me lying helpless
and bloody as you were born.
I could only carry you so far.
My muscles pressed *eject* and then
my cry was not your cry,

while outside who can say what wild
cargo passed us by?

TRANSPORT TO SUMER

When Carolyn was a grad student
at the University of Chicago
she overlapped with Paul Wolfowitz,
architect of the "pre-emptive war" policy,
who was studying under Leo Strauss.
Carolyn was a nun then,
in a medieval habit that brushed the ground
like a medieval angel's wings.
She was called "mother"
after she got her master's.
Lesser nuns (called "sisters")
washed her habits for her.
It was the late '60s,
    and I was a toddler, out West in Seattle,
sleeping with a stuffed tiger
called "Halloweeny."
    Later—in the 1990s—I moved to Chicago
for my Ph.D. I thought knowledge
would make me weighty,
like a "sister," if not a "mother,"
but I stayed myself-growing-older,
and every day I walked past a statue
honoring Enrico Fermi,
who split the atoms that fell
on Hiroshima and Nagasaki.
    When I met Carolyn at an alumni
reception in Milwaukee, we compared notes
about our time at the U. of C.,

    and I wanted to say it changed me
because I met you there, Chris Roth,
and love made my whole body smart
as we sat on a fire escape
listening to the downstairs neighbors
lecture their daughter, Amber,
with fall sweeping Hyde Park involuntarily
setting the trees on fire.
    So, Chris: what's weighty?
Once we visited the U. of C. museum
where they had the Gates of Babylon
propped against one wall,
and clay figures from Sumer

with stick legs and enormous eyes.
The gates were weighty. The Sumerians
were light. Leaves are light. Light
is light. As we age we shrink,
and I am glad to hold you
at night like an archaeological find:
a person who walked with me out of the ruins—
so long Paul Wolfowitz,
ciao to the splitters of atoms.

MUSEUM STUDY

After a pencil drawing, "St. Adolf's Castle," by the self-taught Swiss artist Adolf Wülfli

>–┤◆>•–O•–<◆┤–<

Whatever be the real connection of the words "bear" and "Bern," the figure
of a bear occurs in the oldest known city seal (1224), and living bears have
been kept in Bern at the town's expense since 1513.
MUIRHEAD'S SWITZERLAND, 1923

>–┤◆>•–O•–<◆┤–<

Bern's bears aren't Swiss.
Their brown backs bristle
with mud and burrs.
They don't speak German,
French, or Romansh.
They don't give a rip.
They circle circle circle,
wearing a path in the pit.
Is everything sacred sacred
because it's inaccessible (stars,
deep sea wrecks, Alpenglow)?
The bears won't say if they know.

Meanwhile, Bernese citizens
concentrate on cleaning.
Mothers launder sheets.
Fathers launder gold.
Tourists watch the bears,
barely breathing.

But wait: on a side street,
in Waldau Psychiatric Clinic,
a man with a wolf's name
is penciling a postcard
to the bears. In lieu of the prey
they crave, he draws yellow
doors. Above the doors,
two clocks tick—ten past six,
early twentieth century.
Bears, Bears, open the doors—
if we can dream in color
then the wilderness is ours.

FIRST LADY OF THE WAR

Photograph, 1863

A tourniquet-corset won't cut off the blood
that floods my brain—wave after wave—
but still I cinch my waist, dressing

in skirts with their own musculature,
in shoes that preen my toes to points.
I'm drowning in myself, up to my neck

in Mary Lincoln. A few grapes would soothe
my throat, but there are none in the whole
broken union, unless you count the stuff

our soldiers puke up. All night cotton
bolls roar in my ears. They're meant to blot
out noise but have their own sob stories.

This is my place in history, here in the deep
river, hem wet, high heels not high
enough. I'm cold in my compact body

built for cake and milk. The river runs red
though I am black and white. It pulls
me under and makes me swallow

every sick thing I can't fight.

THE URN

Saltwater:

our cells know we need it,
even if—drifting without looking—
we forget. My Aunt Sigrid's ashes
were sprinkled from an urn
into Puget Sound,

though in life she barked orders
through a megaphone
implanted in her chest.
She drank Folgers coffee,
jolting herself from scandal to scandal,

while her husband parked his sedan
out on the gravel shoulder,
chugging scotch until he turned
into a basset hound,
the kind you see painted on velvet
playing poker.

It's hard to know what made her madder:
Bill Clinton,
rock and roll,
or male homosexual ice skaters.

She irked almost everyone,
which makes her wedding picture a koan,
because there her skin's illumined
like the Sound at sunrise
before the tugs and trawlers rev
their motors. Is it a trick
of sepia light, or are Quakers right
that everyone's born divine?

Thou still unravished
bride of quietness—

the camera's holier than the human
mind: see how it filters out the truth
and leaves the beauty.

DOVE AND DOVE

Côte d'Azur, 1981

Paloma Picasso stands on the high dive wearing a black maillot.
Below her, the photographer forgets the Holy Spirit's ascension

as he plunges into concentration: Paloma is vital—her perfume flies
off shelves all over France. Above the photographer's bent head

a moth unspools its thirty hours of life, extending them unconsciously
until the patio and pool approach immortality. But the sun's

having none such truck: it sails past, a thrown hat, its arc so fast
the photographer curses. Just out of earshot, a girl in a chador

examines her own knee and remembers how the snow in the Pyrenees
—snow she's never seen—flies skyward when the wind is right,

as if everything could gather, at last, in Allah's palm. The photographer
rubs his eyes and thinks about lunch, bread rising, oranges overheating

and falling from a tree in his backyard, how his wife undoes her hair
as she works in the kitchen. She's over fifty, no Paloma,

and yet his mouth waters as he pictures sweat beading on her shoulders,
ready to roll down her back. Then Paloma dives into the pool,

a pool so neutral, so germfree, it's what her father swore heaven
(a place he reviled) would be. "But I'm alive," she said at age five,

lifting her arms as he pushed past on his way to the beach,
where he painted, not the sun, but stronger light: the bright black line

where sea meets sky, where navigators lose themselves at night.
"But I'm alive," Paloma repeats now, changing from crawl to butterfly,

as if she could lift herself eye-level with her father. But no: there's just
the photographer, who, like everyone (so she forgives him) has failed

to capture her.

NOTES

In "Rose," the (misquoted) lines from "Ring of Fire" were written by June Carter Cash and Merle Kilgore.

In "The Urn," the two italicized lines are from John Keats, "Ode on a Grecian Urn."

THE BRITTINGHAM PRIZE IN POETRY
Ronald Wallace, General Editor

Places/Everyone • Jim Daniels
C. K. Williams, Judge, 1985

Talking to Strangers • Patricia Dobler
Maxine Kumin, Judge, 1986

Saving the Young Men of Vienna • David Kirby
Mona Van Duyn, Judge, 1987

Pocket Sundial • Lisa Zeidner
Charles Wright, Judge, 1988

Slow Joy • Stephanie Marlis
Gerald Stern, Judge, 1989

Level Green • Judith Vollmer
Mary Oliver, Judge, 1990

Salt • Renée Ashley
Donald Finkel, Judge, 1991

Sweet Ruin • Tony Hoagland
Donald Justice, Judge 1992

The Red Virgin: A Poem of Simone Weil • Stephanie Strickland
Lisel Mueller, Judge, 1993

The Unbeliever • Lisa Lewis
Henry Taylor, Judge, 1994

Old and New Testaments • Lynn Powell
Carolyn Kizer, Judge, 1995

Brief Landing on the Earth's Surface • Juanita Brunk
Philip Levine, Judge, 1996

And Her Soul Out of Nothing • Olena Kalytiak Davis
Rita Dove, Judge, 1997

Bardo • Suzanne Paola
Donald Hall, Judge, 1998